ARIZONA

A Picture Book to Remember Her by

**CRESCENT BOOKS
NEW YORK**

CLB 1787
© 1987 Colour Library Books Ltd, Guildford, Surrey, England.
Printed and bound in Barcelona, Spain by Cronion, S.A.
All rights reserved.
1987 edition published by Crescent Books, distributed by Crown Publishers, Inc.
ISBN 0 517 62921 6
h g f e d c b a

Before the 1950s, Arizona was a classic example of a nice place to visit, but not so terrific as a place to live. What made the difference between then and now was air conditioning. This is a place where it almost never rains and the sun beats down without mercy. But that's why it's so beautiful and why more than two billion years of geological history is so dazzlingly displayed in the Grand Canyon, the Painted Desert, Monument Valley and the Petrified Forest.

After the air conditioners made it possible to live there comfortably, Arizona got a reputation as a perfect place for retirement and with it, a perception among other Americans that it was a place populated by old folks. The fact is that the median age is under 30 and the state has one of the highest birth rates in the country.

It took more than air conditioning to accomplish that. In 1911, when Arizona was not yet a state, the Federal Government built a dam on the Salt River to irrigate the land in the Phoenix area, creating an oasis that's home to more than half the state's population. Other dams and water projects, including Hoover Dam and Glen Canyon Dam, have given them the water they need to grow and the power that runs the industries that lure as many people there in search of jobs as for the good life in the sun.

A Government explorer once told his employees in Washington that Arizona was completely without value. He was wrong, of course, but that's one reason why 13 different tribes of Indians live there today. More than a quarter of the state is devoted to Indian reservations, possibly because Government officials believed what their explorer told them. They were big on giving the most valueless acres to Indians. But in this case, they were wrong. There is coal under some of that land, and there are white men eager to get at it. But in the 20th century, unlike the 19th when the reservations simply would have been moved, it's up to the tribal councils to decide and, with a few exceptions, the decisions have been to leave things the way they were. And that seems fitting because, as anyone who lives there will tell you proudly, Arizona is the place "where time stands still."

But that's only partly true. Phoenix is 20 times bigger today that it was in 1950, and though still smaller and more faithful to its original Spanish roots, Tucson is growing at almost the same rate.

And why not? It's a terrific place to live. If you have an air conditioner.

Facing page: an aerial view of the Colorado River near Point Sublime.

Previous pages: the jade green of the Colorado River stands out against the muted tones of the Grand Canyon (these pages). This magnificently-carved landscape was created largely by the swift-flowing Colorado River, which began to scour the flat plateau 25 million years ago, cutting through layer after layer of rock. Top: the Navajo Bridge, Marble Canyon, and (above) Marble Canyon Dam. Facing page: (top) Lake Powell near Wahweap Marina, and (bottom) the rugged scenery five miles southwest of Page. Overleaf: a rafting expedition being prepared in Marble Canyon.

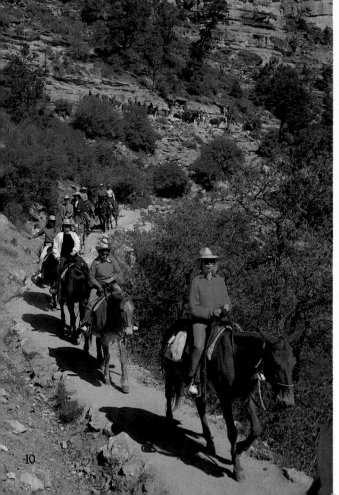

This page: hikers on the Grand Canyon's Bright Angel Trail, which is overlooked by Studio Lookout (facing page top). Facing page bottom: the Colorado River.

A RAINBOW OF COLOR

The Vermilion Cliffs are the remains of once-continuous layers of rock that extended across the entire canyon.

HOW MANY LAYERS CAN YOU IDENTIFY?

NAVAJO: A massive layer of windblown sand, deposited 150 million years ago. Widely distributed, it forms the white cliffs of Zion National Park.

El. 6158 ft.

MOENAVE: A rock layer that contains ripple marks, indicating an ancient stream-bed origin.

CHINLE: These varicolored clay slopes are made of the same formation found at the Painted Desert in Petrified Forest National Park.

SHINARUMP: Another ancient stream-bed deposit. This layer of hard rock provides an important part of the geology story at the next stop.

MOENKOPI: These sediments are probably ancient tidal mudflats. Iron oxide has added the splash of color.

RIVER DEPOSITS: Stream gravel, rock debris and sand, recent in origin, mantle most of the nearby formations.

Previous pages: the Battleship, seen from Pima Point, and (top, left and facing page top) land around Marble Canyon (remaining pictures), in the Grand Canyon.

14

Previous pages: Havasu Falls, an oasis of greenery in the arid Grand Canyon, and (top) the 726-foot-high Hoover Dam at Lake Mead. Facing page: (bottom) the stern-wheeler *River Queen* moored at London Bridge (top), (above) nearby English Village, and (right) Lake Havasu Golf Course, all at Lake Havasu City, southwest of the Grand Canyon, on the Colorado River.

Throughout the spring, much of the Grand Canyon is adorned with bright cactus flowers, including (top) hedgehog cactus, (left) grizzly bear prickly pear, and (above) beaver tail prickly pear cactus. Facing page: a fine specimen at Organ Pipe Cactus National Monument in the southwest, by the Mexican border.

![Wells Fargo Museum signs and storefront with "Jewelry Making" sign and stagecoach with "Wells Fargo Museum Entrance" text](full-page-top-image)

Above: a stagecoach on Allen Street, (right) the Court House and (remaining pictures) museums and novelty stores, all in historic Tombstone. During the lawless days of the 19th-century silver and gold mining boom, this became "the town too tough to die," famed for the Earps - Clanton gun battle at the O.K. Corral.

Previous pages: (left top) the Kitt Peak National Observatory and (left bottom and right top) giant cactii at the Saguaro National Monument, both west of Tucson, and (right bottom) Mission San Jose de Tumacacori, north of Nogales. Top: Pima County Court House, (right) Congress Street, and (remaining pictures) United Bank Plaza, all in Tucson, Arizona's second city and a major center for tourism.

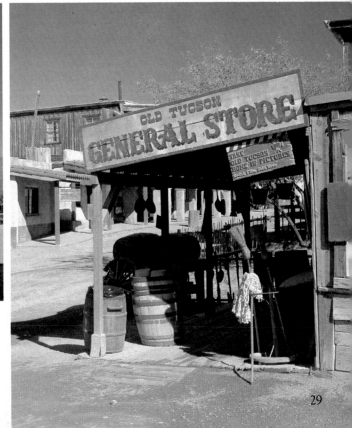

In 1940 Columbia Pictures constructed a frontier town just west of Tucson for their film *Arizona*. It was also used for the television series *High Chaparral* before becoming one of the area's main tourist attractions as Old Tucson (these pages). The set now offers such features as an antique carousel, museums, stagecoach rides and frequent gunfights.

Previous pages: among Tucson's many attractions are (left bottom) the beautiful Mission San Xavier Del Bac, which is known as the "White Dove of the Desert" and has been ministering to the Papagos Indians since it was built in 1782, (left top) the University of Arizona campus, (right top) a view from Sentinel Peak towards Tucson Mountain Park, which can be reached via Gates Pass (right bottom). Facing page: (top) the Santa Catalina Mountains, northeast of Tucson, (bottom) saguaro cactus in the desert near Phoenix, Arizona's capital, and (above) the Pinal County Building at Florence, southeast of Phoenix.

Facing page bottom, right and overleaf right bottom:
the Valley Bank Center in downtown Phoenix, (facing
page top and overleaf left top) the State Capitol,
(above) Rosson House in Heritáge Square, and (top)
Phoenix Civic Plaza, overlooked by St. Mary's Church
(overleaf left bottom) and featuring Jerome Kirk's
sculpture *Phoenix Bird Ascending* (overleaf right top).

Top: buildings on Central Avenue in downtown Phoenix, (left) the grounds of the City Hall (above) of Scottsdale, a large and fashionable suburb of Phoenix centered around Old Scottsdale (facing page top). Facing page bottom: sculpture on Scottsdale Mall, and (overleaf) the nearby leisure center, Boulders.

The northwest face of the Santa Catalina Mountains forms a rugged backdrop to Catalina State Park (previous pages), north of Tucson. Covering 5,500 acres of the land once inhabited by the Hohokam Indians, this fascinating park contains an extensive variety of desert plants and wildlife. Above: a view from Highway 666, near Nutrioso, of a tranquil lake in the hills of Apache National Forest, through which flows the East Fork of the Black River (left and facing page top), and (facing page bottom) views across this area of east-central Arizona towards Springerville. Overleaf: (left bottom) the Highway 60 Bridge spanning the Salt River (left top), at Salt River Canyon in San Carlos Indian Reservation, and (right) Tonto National Monument, near the Theodore Roosevelt Lake in south-central Arizona. This remarkable monument preserves the remains of a two-story cliff dwelling that was built by the Salado Indians over 700 years ago.

Petrified Forest National Park, near
Holbrook in eastern Arizona,
contains one of the world's largest
concentrations of petrified wood (top).
The logs are around 160 million years
old and slowly became impregnated
with solutions of silica and mineral
deposits that turned them into richly-
colored boulders. To the north of the
forest, stretching nearly 200 miles to
the Grand Canyon, is the remarkable
Painted Desert (left and facing page
bottom), where the sculptured forms of
stratified rock lie in bands of rainbow
hues. Facing page top: Meteor Crater,
near Winslow, which was formed by a
falling meteorite over 22,000 years
ago, and (overleaf) pine, juniper and
cypress trees add to the soft colors of
the cliffs and buttes at Oak Creek
Canyon, near Sedona.

Jerome (top), an old mining town in the mountains northeast of Prescott, was largely depopulated when its copper mines were closed in the 1950s. Its history is now featured in Jerome State Historic Park (above and left). Facing page: (top) the Granite Dells near Prescott, and (bottom) the Spanish-Colonial-style town of TlaquePaque, built near Sedona in the 1970s.

Previous pages: (left top) Gurley Street in downtown Prescott, and (left bottom) Arconsanti, near Cordes Junction, a "city of the future" designed, by architect Paolo Soleri, to accommodate living and working facilities for about 5,000 people. Looking way back into the past, several Indian cliff-dwellings are to be found around Beaver Creek (right top), in Coconino National Forest, south of Flagstaff, one of the best-preserved being Montezuma Castle National Monument (right bottom), which dates from the 12th-13th centuries. Left: Sedona, which enjoys spectacular surroundings at the southern end of Oak Creek Canyon (remaining pictures), in the scenic Red Rocks area. Below: babbling, trout-filled Oak Creek at Red Rocks Crossing.

Previous pages: snow on the San Francisco Peaks in the Arizona Snow Bowl ski area, where an 11,600-foot-high elevation affords breathtaking views of five states. Straddling the border with Utah in eastern Arizona is Monument Valley Navajo Tribal Park, a vast desert best known for its massive sandstone monoliths (right), which include the distinctive Mitten Buttes (facing page bottom). Above: dramatic formations at Canyon de Chelly in the state's northeasterly reaches. Still the home of the Navajo, this valley has been cultivated by successive Indian tribes since about A.D. 350. Among its principal remaining ruins is the White House (facing page top and overleaf left bottom), which was occupied between 1060 and 1275. Another interesting feature is slender Spider Rock (overleaf left top). Overleaf: (right top) West Mitten, East Mitten and Merrick Butte, (right bottom) West Mitten, and (following page) Mitchell Butte, all in Monument Valley Navajo Tribal Park.

61